PROUD ROADS
KELLY RIEDESEL

LOBLOLLY PRESS

MILO-PIMÂTISÎWIN

"GOOD LIFE"

There is no direct analogue for "Proud Roads" in Moose Cree, though in my Nation's language Michif (the Métis language) we have two words that capture a similar meaning:

Miyo // Good // mi-yo
Piimaatishiiwin // Life // pi-maa-tish-ee-win

In Moose Cree, spoken by the Mushkegowuk, this can come together as Milo-pimâtisîwin—Good Life. It carries the teaching of living in balance: physically, emotionally, mentally, and spiritually connected to yourself, your family, community, nature, and the spiritual world.

It's a way of making meaning in the world, to live in a good way, with respect and understanding for the generations that have come before you. It's also to live in a way that generations after you can live in a good way too.

Importantly, for *Proud Roads* there is resilience in balanced living, meaning that even in hardship, you choose to walk in a way that creates hope, healing, and strength for yourself and others.

ᒥᔪ ᐱᒫᑎᓯᐃᐧᐣ. Milo-pimâtisîwin. Proud Roads.

Published by Loblolly Press
loblollypress.com
Asheville, NC

Copyright © 2025 by Kelly Riedesel

All rights reserved. No part of this publication may be reproduced, distributed, or transmitted in any form by any means, including photocopying, recording, or other electronic methods without the prior written permission of the author, except in the case of brief quotations embodied in reviews and certain other noncommercial uses permitted by copyright law. For permission requests, write to the publisher at: permissions@loblollypress.com

Cover design by Emma Ensley @emma_ensley
Photographs from Kelly Riedesel @kellyriedesel
Interior design by Andrew Mack @andrewmack_poetry

Instagram: @loblolly_press
Newsletter: loblollypress.substack.com

Paperback ISBN: 979-8-9900730-8-1
Printed in the United States of America

First Printing, September 2025

For belonging *with*, not to –

and for Todd Nathaniel Swift, always with,
whose untimely passing prompted me to finally share my
poetry

CONTENTS

SEPTEMBER

5 PREPAREDNESS
7 DISASTER ROAMING
8 BLOOD OATH
9 APPALACHIAN HOMECOMING

OCTOBER

13 ALCHEMY
16 MUD IN OUR EYES
17 MULES COME WALKING
18 WATER LEVELS
19 HAUNTING
20 SOLVING FOR X
22 VESSEL
23 MIRROR
24 CHALLENGING ANXIOUS THOUGHTS
26 KINSHIP WÂHKÔHTOWIN
27 DIGNITY

NOVEMBER

31 THE WARNING
32 DISPLACEMENT
33 LIVING EPITAPH
34 TEMPERATURE
35 FALLOW
36 DAY OF CROWS SEPTEMBER 27, 2024
37 PRODIGAL
38 SPEECHLESS
40 EXPECTATIONS

DECEMBER–JANUARY

45 TOLL ROADS
46 DAY OF REST
48 TRUST
49 100 DAYS
50 PROUD ROADS
51 IT'S EVERYTHING
53 BELONGING
55 WÂWÂŠTESKWAN THE SPIRITS DANCING

PROUD ROADS

ᒥᔪ ᐱᒫᑎᓯᐃᐧᐣ

MILO–PIMÂTISÎWIN

SEPTEMBER

This extreme amount of rain over already-saturated soils resulted in catastrophic and historic flooding across western North Carolina. In the city of Asheville, North Carolina, some likened this flood event to that of the "Great Flood" of 1916. The river gauge along the French Broad River in Asheville exceeded the previous record of the 1916 flood by over 1.5 feet at the peak of Helene's flooding. Several other rivers in the surrounding area, such as the Swannanoa River at Biltmore, also set new records. All this rainfall also caused intense stress to the mountainous terrain, and nearly 2,000 total landslides have been observed according to the United States Geological Survey. At one point, all roads in western North Carolina were considered closed to all non-emergency travel.

This event is close to, if not a worse-case scenario meteorologically speaking, for western North Carolina. The full extent of the damages is still being realized and will take months to years to document and recover from.

— "Hurricane Helene's Extreme Rainfall and Catastrophic Inland Flooding", Haley Thiem and Rebecca Lindsey, Event Tracker, Climate.gov, November 7, 2024.

PREPAREDNESS

Helene made a mockery of civilization today.

All night, I heard trees shatter, splinter, explode
and crash to the ground,
the standing ones,
huge hundred-year-old Elders,
fell one by one,
roots ripped from crust

now fan blades
poking out at odd angles
from saturated clay hollows,

where once there was green forest.
Now there are gaping holes
filled with sky

Helene made a flashlight
out of my cell phone,
deadly snakes out of power lines

somehow our bridge,
our lifeline,
was spared

all day,
we neighbors labored under now sunny skies
to unearth our lives

Rooftop rescues from raging waters,
lifeboats looking like fish flopping on land
out of breath

by evening
birds congregate in the one tall tree left in my yard,
filling the air above my house with bitter concerns

once the sun set,
there were no more human sounds
no lights

only screeching crickets, shrilling katydids,
the trickling of hundreds of new rivulets of water
across broken land that was never indestructible

now every gust of wind,
every snapping branch,
makes me startle inside and out

I cannot sleep knowing many have no beds,
no shelter,
not knowing where their kin may be

The night dogs howl their names.

DISASTER ROAMING

Disaster roaming has been enacted:
connection granted to any working tower.

    Crews are disaster roaming from near and far,
    even French Canadians—restoring light to our town.

The governor and mayors, flanked by disaster relief,
roam the skies in helicopters, naming what they cannot mend.

    People are disaster roaming the open roadways:
    on scooters, bikes, and borrowed wheels,

to reach donation stations rising from parking lots,
hoping for water, bread, insulin, humanity, a charge.

    Some are disaster roaming toward hospitals,
    the fortunate ones begin chemo alone.

Animals disaster roam,
cows in ditches, dogs in fields, pigs among splinters.

    Even the clouds are disaster roaming:
    casting a pall over traumatized people.

Survivors disaster roam,
using borrowed signals to call in the dead.

BLOOD OATH

Take heart, the oath stands
even given the cataclysmic damage
of mountain rain funnels and wind tunnels,
it stands, even as we toil for repair

Start in spring when winter's gray melts,
sustaining the release of bright green buds on a trillion branches
Sit in white dogwood flower floating cups in scattered sunlight
on steep slopes gathering time

Fold into summer's lush fields
days filled with yellow light
knowing there is no end to mindful harvest
In the growing warm breezes
inhale the bonds of generations

As with the rest of nature,
yield,
as the days get shorter—drink,
as the trees' red leaves
offer their annual renewal of our blood oath
before winter's edge,
tip the cup up

APPALACHIAN HOMECOMING

It's getting late
the witching hour
when the windows blacken with sunset.

It's getting dark
when the precious distraction of physical work must stop
and all the held-back ache begins.

I return from the grocery store
still running on a generator,
with a single slice of tiramisu for his birthday tomorrow.

We meet in a nearby parking lot.
The van too tall
to slip beneath the fallen power lines to home.

I step out of the car.
He does a little dance—
like a puppy,

but when I reach to touch him,
he collapses onto my shoulders,
his body all salt and gravity.

I cannot hold him up.
He slips against the side of the car,
finally letting go.

I start to speak, but no.
He heaves the days of burdens,
what the storm refused to spare.

This is one version of homecoming after Helene,
one of thousands.
We are the lucky ones.

OCTOBER

Last month Hurricane Camille struck and destroyed homes, factories, and sometimes, entire towns. This left thousands homeless, penniless, and without any clothing. The American public responded with incredible generosity in giving food and clothing, so much so that now there is a surplus in these commodities.

Unfortunately, you cannot rebuild houses with ham and peas or bury loved ones with clothes. These things can only be accomplished with money, lots of money.

— "HELP!!!" David Sullian, *The Echo*, Warren Wilson College, 1969.

They didn't have any estimates on when basic services might be restored. The lack of water was our main concern. Our next-door neighbors were drinking the water from their hot water heater. Others were gathering water from the creek. We started boiling the rainwater we'd collected in two five-gallon buckets.

— "A Disaster No One Saw Coming" Storms Reback, Theassemblync.com, October 2, 2024.

ALCHEMY

*Fear is turning into cooperation for those who have just enough,
and into more fear for those that don't.*

I wake

to a new alchemy
resources managed by we the people
most with no power or water,
mixed with plenty of anxiety,
hope, a strand in the wind

Chain saws buzz desires

I learn

four of my neighbors are climate refugees,
their homes destroyed,
they nest with family elsewhere

I want

decaying dinosaur bodies
to run my generator –
to run my well pump –
to provide precious drinking water

I want

to know what has happened
outside my still-running home

I learn

county emergency services leaders
can barely hold a Zoom meeting
communications are so sketchy

I listen

but they know so little,
tell me nothing about what I need to know,
help is coming they say

I learn

their focus is on saving lives
not managing existence
or existential threats

I feel

like it's Covid 2.0,
everyone awaiting
an uncertainty vaccine

I stand

by as my brave neighbor
cuts the downed power lines blocking
our egress to the new world

I offer

hot showers to his family
his tween daughter emerges, hair washed,
her gratefulness shines in her slight smile and brighter eyes

I offer

drinking water and bathroom access
to my neighbor who always grades the road after storms

He offers

spotty cell phone service to contact my husband,
a nurse on 24-hour mayhem duty,
sleeping in the nursing home parking lot

I want

to know if he's safe and if he might
be able to bring home survival in a gas can
when the siege calms.

He doesn't know, nobody knows.
He cannot leave such vulnerable patients anyway.
I slept last night, finally.

I wake, I stay

underground for another hour,
considering the wisdom of getting up
to greet the day

What might I do that really matters
except sit tight,
stay out of the way
of inching dinosaurs.

MUD IN OUR EYES

10 days ago.
world lifted. carried. buried.
water. funneling. barreling.
our beings. blended. drowned.

ears reveal. whimpers from receding flows.
hands sink. reach deep for hands.
under landslides, poking out.
mouths taste. muddy vomit from lungs.
noses smell. fetid home.
heart blood. mud displaced.

we souls. barely survived.
savor what's left.
our eyes. burned images.
one day our mouths
tasting solidarity will shout:
"Here's mud in your eye!"

MULES COME WALKING

Mules come walking bringing us home.
They carry the mountain, shoulders like stone.
When mules come walking, despair becomes known.
Mules come walking, muscle and bone.
Mules haul our survival, their strength our light
They bring supplies into our deepening night.
The mules are faithful, the muletary is now fabled.
That's why mules get utmost respect at the stable.
So, if you spy mules where roads turn to scree,
best hush your voice, just watch and see.
The mules will muster, and you'll get the honor
of seeing the mules go over the holler.

WATER LEVELS

1

Helene's rain leveled
what we thought was permanent.
Life that gathered water,
now water gathering lives
indiscriminately.

2

Humble water:
jobs, homes, hospitals, farmsteads,
restaurants, schools, libraries, art
all folded like gossamer cloth
introducing us to ourselves.

3

Water behind dams
cools nuclear reactors,
water in glaciers melting
bound to cloud ash particles,
does what only water can.

4

Helene's rain leveled
the things we counted on
to do the life we counted
on that counts on water,
humble water.

HAUNTING

Today the haints surrounded me
through loaded questions at the reception desk

Name?
this is my name, but I am not the same

Address the same?
it does not look like home anymore

Phone number the same?
do not call to me from beyond

Knowing haints cannot move across water,
I go wash my hands in the dirty tap,
these loaded questions haunting my mind.
I wonder if haint blue jars of mud could suffice.

SOLVING FOR X

X =
Lethal,
the front door spray paint mark
marks the spot of search and rescue teams
people found alive and dead.
I can't. I just can't.

X =
Vexing,
more complex than an algebraic equation
is solving for the search and rescue X code
marked on the front door of my mind

X =
Needles,
now that geologic time has reached me
time struggles to teach me that
it will heal all wounds,
wounds marked with an X

X=
Feeble,
muddling to identify what I feel,
the difference between sad and afraid,
angry and dismayed,
a piece of my mind for peace of mind

X =
Upheaval,
new landslides of what's missing,
old parting words of
Be safe!,
replaced by pleas of
Stay safe!

X =
Brutal,
the sum of all the X's on all the doors I can't unsee
that are blocking my view,
the solution to this double substitution problem

X =
Fetal,
rocking with the distress long enough
to solve for what's missing,
substituting it back into my soul
to solve for all the unknowns

X =
Primeval,
braving the wind
until it no longer takes my breath away

X =
Unequal,
doing old life in a new way
doing new life in an old way
the uncertainty becoming more acceptable
as the path to what I value most,
who I want to be regardless of circumstance

X =
Peaceful,
tracing my son's childhood handprint,
remembering how clear and calm the water was
at my favorite swimming hole,
touching the delicate petals
of small flowers blooming on creek banks,
counting my dog's eyelashes in the morning sunlight
as he blinks his affection

VESSEL

She comes with every available vessel
to fill with water from our well,
harnessing Nature's plenty,
the She from which we live

She is the vessel conveying water
to survivors who have none,
forming new bonds:
with stunned and vacant faces

In a world obsolete of "How are you?"
The vessel speaks to survivors
greeting them:
"You okay? You need water?"

MIRROR

The Helene mirror is for making stone
It shows us our desires

        Dire need desires reasons
        Desperately peeking at Medusa

We peak for absolution
A reprieve from beastly climate shame

        She brings her beastly defiance closer
        Her resources – no flinching, no wincing

More resources aren't the answer
to right what is wrong here

        The empty right that does all wrongs
        Reflections on ambition, contrition

Bleak reflections after the storm
The Helene mirror is for making stone

CHALLENGING ANXIOUS THOUGHTS

After so many years of disability I had gotten good at this
I could walk back a worst-case scenario in my sleep
could answer the doom in my mind with logic
with calm
with slowing down my reactions to responses I knew
how to test a thought for evidence
how to heap falsehood on
the distortion pile of visceral demise
how to pile certain matters into stacks
to see if they would still matter in a week
a month
a year
ten years from now
how to harness that most things pass
that I'd been here before
that I would be okay

but then Helene's second flood came in evidence
came in doors came under houses and above roofs
came in dirty creek water to wash dishes the evidence
washed away interstate highways
came in hospitals on life support mothers carrying their kids
down ladders on their backs across washed out riverbeds to find
shelter from avalanches that spun humans as if in rock tumblers and kids
kids walking along a country road half naked unable to find their parents
the evidence came in of no power no showers whole
apartment blocks of elderly with no oxygen or mobility there
are bodies found counties away from their origins the questions
the questions are the flood and the flood of questions my mind can't keep up with

the worst-case scenario is no longer my personal distortion it's
omnipotent and everywhere in everyone

it is statistically undeniable
it is laws of nature Newton's motion of industrial inertia
it is the entire mass of the earth the amount of force we apply to it
is in satellite images
rewritten maps with red zones and black flags
is in extreme weather text alerts and emergency shelter warnings
is in the eyes of children who have new rules for survival

I thought I was the Olympic champion
of challenging anxious thoughts
but now I am salt dissolving in the sullied broth of flood water
no question I can ask to recrystallize my strength

but in this mire of uncertainty a new answer has emerged
built day by day by
hands lifting lives branch by branch
hour by hour by
hearts offering humanity to the weary
minute by minute by
children watching what care looks like

these are the things
that will still matter in a week
a month
a year
ten years from now

the practice not of managing fear
but naming the hands that carry us through it

this
this is what challenges anxious thoughts in a world
disabled, still alive

KINSHIP WÂHKÔHTOWIN

Kinship was already growing here, among relatives,
out of the ground like medicine
like the Haudenosaunee thanksgiving address given on Cherokee land
with words before all else, and nothing to prove

out of the ground like medicine
not perfect just perfectly practiced
with words before all else, and nothing to prove
remembering the duty to move in balance and harmony

not perfect just perfectly practiced
no creature more important than another, each with its own job
remembering the duty to move in balance and harmony
reminding us that kinship starts with the gathering of good mind and heart

no creature more important than another, each with its own job
offering gratitude and thanks for every living thing
reminding us that kinship starts with the gathering good mind and heart
toward one disaster mindset for all

offering gratitude and thanks for every living thing
not taken for granted, else it would not have grown
toward one disaster mindset for all
so the cycle of life can continue

not taken for granted, else it would not have grown
like the Haudenosaunee thanksgiving address given on Cherokee land
so the cycle of life can continue.
Kinship was already growing here, among relatives.

DIGNITY

Please do not forget in a month or a year
that Dignity was buried here.

You do not need to witness the destruction
everywhere you go every day
to understand
that pride is not supplied at distribution centers,
that tent walls do not provide confidence,
that public showers do not offer privacy,
that burials must be sacred,
that dignity comes not from taking what crumbs are offered
but from offering what is needed most.

Until Dignity has a front porch for reciprocity,
its burial in clothes no more,
we will have ham and peas stuck in our throats.

NOVEMBER

It is said that Americans pull together in the wake of disaster. I have seen it after hurricanes, during Covid-19 and in the moments after a school shooting. We are divided. We are competitors for capitalistic spoils. We are often enemies. But something about a natural disaster calls to our shared humanity.

That is what I have seen since Hurricane Helene. All the disinformation and destruction aside, my friends and colleagues who were in the storm's path have drawn on the community that makes the South my home. Appalachian people, in particular, are proud of helping one another survive.

— "How to Help Those Still Devastated by Hurricane Helene", Tressie McMillan Cottom, nytimes.com, November 27, 2024.

THE WARNING

You call across the valley
as if you are the shepherd—
but your voice does not settle
like safety in the bones of the flock.
It startles. It fractures.

You dress your warnings in urgency,
but your words are vapor
rising from hot air.
Still, the sheep look up.
Still, the village listens.

Each time you ring the bell
with no truth beneath it,
you leave the herd more brittle,
the hillside more hollow.

You are not guardianship.
You are erosion—
of trust, of time, of the thread
that binds us to one another.

You proclaim vigilance.
You proclaim conviction.
But the wolf does not parse
motive from meat.
When it comes,
it will not care
who held the crook
and who wore the wool.

DISPLACEMENT

It's like living in a dream out there
in a world seemingly untouched
by existential dread.
It's hard to look people in the eye
and not warn them to run.

I want to exhibit our shattered legs
standing in line waiting for water, food, shelter,
standing beside white boards waiting for news of the missing,
standing so others have the strength to stand.

I want to brandish our children's faces, prematurely aged,
sullen again like Covid times,
scared as their minds fill with fears facts can't replace,
spooked seeing their fathers cry for the first time.

I want to transmit how our roads home have been rendered,
their flesh at the bottom of chasms,
their skeletons lay like chalk outlines,
land rescue replaced by the constant whirring of helicopters

I want them to know
that staying here is extinction,
leaving feels like betrayal,
there's no escape from this hell.

Forces of nature like displacement
are broken.

LIVING EPITAPH

Our response belies hurricane category
people who know say it's true

We endeavor to recreate the freedom to live
not just be alive

Honor our experience
the withering pain

See red, see blue,
see u.s., unbroken.

TEMPERATURE

Fire's scalding came in the middle of the night
evacuation orders barked in the dark,
instinct shielding senses,
flee compressed by backdraft,
then dawn, an afterburn laced with
"They should have been more prepared!"

                                        Oh the water is hot and we are in it,
                        we panic, swimming in circles as the shore recedes,
                                            we are scavengers by day,
                                            lugging water home in our lungs,
                                        our legs treading on in our dreams,
                                                      all action fluid

The earth is lukewarm now,
our dilemmas full of not knowing what's left to work with,
what can be done, what to do first,
what's worth trying with limited resources,
every toehold with unknown consequences and compromise,
not indifferent, just barely warm enough to have ideas at all

                                                          The air was cool,
                                  as if it absorbed the icy feelings of loss,
                                        loss of every type of infrastructure
                                              like the loss of a parent too soon
                     creating a world we live in but don't understand,
                                                     words just forming

Move, but gently,
the heart is especially vulnerable
protect yourself from the winds
insulate yourself from the ground
take off wet clothing
apply warmth,
it's freezing here.

FALLOW

This fall the valleys are not being left fallow
to kill weeds
or make the soil richer,
or disrupt pest life cycles
in the name of allowing the soil
to become fertile again,
or the pastures to renew in spring.

Where fields that nourished once stood
cultivated by hands that know good work
now lie crushed tractors half buried in mud,
barn boards poking up like stalks in plow lines,
furniture standing like cows in the fields.

What nurtured was plowed under
by Mother Nature herself,
the soil now uncultivable.
The tillable must now be left untilled
as it is filled with tine breaking trash,
the toil of generations silently rotting.

But, in the mountains,
beyond the landslides,
there has always been a nourishing place,
a fallow place of rest
unseeded with deadly traps of efficiency,
barren of life's modern pace,
a place that provides for incremental becoming,
the growing of aliveness,
the cultivation of creation
of all that is enriching and sustaining,
grown to feed the spirit
and allow it to become fertile again.

DAY OF CROWS SEPTEMBER 27, 2024

A murder of crows were cawing for our attention.
Old spirits carrying knowledge from past lifetimes.
Retelling our story.

Their nests blown from the tops of trees.
Their rest on power lines denied.
They circled, landing eventually in yards.

They are deliverers of messages between the worlds.
They await the end of days for sustenance.
They are a reminder of mortality.
They look beyond the obvious toward creative solutions.
They cultivate cooperation and collaboration.
They stick together to protect themselves.
They call instinct and inner voice to action.

There will always be a kinship among survivors.
With those who walked on that day.
Their gift of "It could have been you"
Reminding us to remember who we are.

We are all part crow.

PRODIGAL

some trees
can't be

broken
by

rotting
bootstraps

suddenly weighing
in their branches

SPEECHLESS

Needs have echoed for weeks—
on radios, screens, urgent voices
rising like floodwater.
So many needs met
leaders are left
speechless with gratitude.

But I've seen too much,
heard too much,
held too much.

Now I crave the quiet
of the deer
who move like a memory
through new thickets,

I want the hush of bears
walking fallen trunks
like bridges across what's broken,

Or the soft sway of turkeys
rewriting their trails
through the woods.

The hawk still circles.
The creek still runs,
muddy but speaking.

But I sit
immobile and speechless,
facing the road where a house once was,
the school, the garden,
the names I no longer say aloud.

Not out of fear—
but out of respect
for what still breathes,
for what remains unspeakable
and sacred.

EXPECTATIONS

Remember

Remember

See and remember

With no roads
we'll go together,
stay with me

The world is starting
to have expectations
jobs, bills, time

Let them breathe

Whether we are okay
is entirely the wrong question

See your soul departed
from bricks and mortar.
Exhale the stage.

The right question is,
"Can the expectations wait?"

Let them wait
Your soul has to fathom time
Your soul has to need what's kind
Your soul has to need mine

You have to see what's gone behind
my walls so thick
and my heart so mine

one degree of separation is all it takes
for expectations to flood in,
a land so far from ties that bind
then we are far again from
your soul has to need mine

Turn your soul into an ocean,
let me swim into your sea

The worst of me
needs to protect myself from you
I can't let my guard down
it's what would undo
the last line of defense
I have against losing myself
in your ocean

Your soul has to fathom time
Your soul has to need what's kind
Your soul has to need mine

Remember the freedom
of not knowing time.
I'm afraid of needing your soul.
Your soul has to need mine.

Remember

Remember

See and remember

DECEMBER - JANUARY

Nonprofit BeLoved Asheville has purchased a roughly 8-acre parcel in Swannanoa with plans to build a new "village" of deeply affordable homes, replicating ongoing work at its East Asheville property where 12 tiny homes are awaiting final steps.

— "BeLoved Asheville buys Swannanoa property with plans for new deeply affordable 'village'", Sarah Honosky, Citizen-times.com, Jan 14, 2025.

TOLL ROADS

Working for pay is returning for some,
but the roads we take
take something from us.

The toll is another day of the drive.
The toll is silence between exits.
The toll is driving past the same detour,
still hoping it's gone.

The toll is white knuckles on the wheel.
The toll is driving the gauntlet of the byways.
The toll is there are no red lights for catching a breath.

The toll is the place you used to work
turned to rubble.
The toll is forgetting how you got there.
The toll is opening the door to like-minded co-workers.

The toll is charging mental health days
to vacation time.
The toll is the voice in your head
saying, *be grateful*.

DAY OF REST

Too much, too fast, too soon, too long

Sunday has often been called the day of rest
after disintegration and imbalances fragment
God laid down his hand
and rested from creating creation

When Creator shows us life lies in a circle, the drum beats,
you, born in the east, before words & hands,
listening for where oxygen is needed
to integrate fire's instinct with understanding

For survivors today is the tenth day of recreating
what Helene made unrecognizable
resources laid bare

in the south, cooperation arises
through acknowledging our interdependency
defiantly present

Though our work has differed vastly
we have all been first responders

in the west, we have contributed our gifts,
sacred responsibility given completely

Now we rest,

in the north, we rise like smoke,

we honor each other's beliefs   our truths reclaiming our spirits
For the many still missing,   we hold ceremony, we remember,
there is no rest for their beloveds   we keep the fire burning

We make every day holy   we become the fire again, we listen again,
by honoring each other with our presence   we are the drum story

Humanity is what is recognizable now, the rest doesn't matter anymore

TRUST

Trust comes one lab result, one story, one sip at a time,
promises kept, no disasters left, no slips, not resigned.
No absolutes turned on a dime.

After scouring, drought, and lead warnings combined,
tap water comes with suspicion.
Trust comes one lab result, one story, one sip at a time.

After reservoir water mucky with slime,
infrastructure and economy on fragile lifelines.
No absolutes turned on a dime.

After weeks of creek water used for toilet prime,
and bathwater so suspect parents decline.
Trust comes one lab result, one story, one sip at a time.

After months of waiting on everyone's minds,
survival in a bottle the daily find.
No absolutes turned on a dime.

After lives already spared once by water's crime, belief for survivors
is a verb.
Trust comes one lab result, one story, one sip at a time.
No absolutes turned on a dime.

100 DAYS

I could write about what has been accomplished
these one hundred days since the storm,
the heroic work of thousands,
the love of millions,
covering survivors in a patchwork quilt of fabric hugs,
cherished like a grandmother's handiwork.

I could write much more about what has not been accomplished,
the failures of governments with their heavy limbs,
pages of processes fabricated from downed trees,
the leaves no longer able to provide people with oxygen,
invisible anyway, like all gases.

I could write about how the post-disaster honeymoon phase is over
how much help has sublimated
like snowfall on a zero-humidity day,
how disheartening that is
when the snow on the branches was so beautiful.

All I can say about the balance
between disillusionment and reconstruction
is that it is not linear or sequential.
It is happening one day at a time.
It is messy, very messy.

We have no practice, no manual.
We are all learning to ride a bike for the first time,
feeling the wind in our hair
while balancing precariously over the bumps in the sidewalk,
not at all ready for the training wheels to come off.

PROUD ROADS

Caring people live on proud roads,
roads held together by doing the one thing
that's always been available and free.

Along the highways that Helene erased,
governments put conditions on assistance,
insurance companies find reasons not to pay,
media moves on to the next story.
But along the double track dirt roads
and holler footpaths we cut ourselves,
caring has no bounds.

Our caring is what makes you want to visit,
where you're made to feel like part of the family,
where we still craft things by hand,
sentimental heirlooms,
that help you remember how our caring felt
once you get back on the highway.

Right now, we have to say, don't come here.
We are knee-deep doing what only we can do,
because we are the people
who will inherit that proud.

We are flooding back love,
standing up when we can, without comment,
sitting down when we must, without guilt,
doing the things that keep us proud.

Caring people live on proud roads,
that reasons cannot reach.

IT'S EVERYTHING

   It's a challenging childhood
         it's military service during wartime
                it's the death of my dad
                        it's five miscarriages
                                it's disabilities
it's loss of livelihood
      it's searing surgeries
             it's a failing medical system
                    it's the death of my mom during a pandemic
it's finding family nearly too late
      it's the second election of a bully.

it's an epic natural disaster
         that is every disaster I've ever been through
                it's every fallen tree
                        it's every pile of debris
                              it's every road washed away
it's every bridge that gave way
      it's every home torn from its foundation
             it's every bedrock annihilation
                    it's everything eviscerating me again.

It's all there for my eyes to see
      what on my heart's emblazoned
                Time's erasure of my red fingerprints from buried fetal
bodies
                the wrinkles from strangers' assumptions

the futile mapping of my feet
      the scalpel's imprints under the surface
             the marks of Care's impudence on my spirit
                    the longing for DNA's stories from every cell

It's everything that made me a narrative beast
an equal beast to being gutted at least
the owner of my story's swords
the creator of the battle between fear and love,
creator of what gets to pluck the chords,
creator of the place I arrive at when push comes to shove.
It's everything landslides bring.

BELONGING

  I've been in love with water my whole life,
as a child, playing in the neighborhood stream,
   lying in storm gutters, the water rushing over me,
     gathering gigantic icicles off the roof,
       wading in the ocean next to my home overseas,
         then becoming a master of water science,
           a career protecting the water,
             later taking my son to play in the creek below our house,
            sitting and crying next to lakes in moments of despair,
          the water bringing my unconscious thoughts to the surface for repair,
       its capacity to absorb my woes in its depths never failing,
    flowing in and out of each other's banks,
   our mutual support never wavering,
  I felt we belonged to each other.
All of that was before I knew about being Métis,
my fur trading ancestral family defined themselves through water,
   their economic, social and cultural fabric evolved on water highways.
     Before the Métis, my family was Moose Cree from James Bay,
        ice fishing, goose hunting, stewardship of nature for arctic survival,
          the spiritual significance of water
          as clear as the water itself, the belonging sacred.
When half a year's worth of rain fell in three days,
  I was spared its worst wrath, but felt forsaken somehow,
    the water sullied with every manner of pollution,
      looking disavowed of my love, dead to us,
        leaving me wondering how our bonds could be drowned overnight
          when our connection had been thousands of years in the making.
       That day, water showed me its whole true self, leaving me no illusions,
      leaving me with a decision about belonging. Who disavowed who?
     Had I demanded an idyllic version of water that is no longer true,
   or required the removal of some of its parts in order for it to belong to me?

Belonging shouldn't depend on an illusion.
    I belong not to a certain version of water,
        but with water as it is, and with all that keeps happening to
            water every day.
                We belong when our becoming is included in our love.
          I'll always belong with water now, wrapped in its ancestral
      cycles as it has been with mine,
        I will open my mouth to catch acidic snowflakes,
       see rain as the bringer of life as well as death,
     allow falling water to rush over me even if it drowns me,
   steward the water with my bare hands,
walk into creeks in my bare feet,
    wade into surfers' ocean waves,
        drink water's sullied molecules into my blood,
          carry its richness and its sorrows,
              washed in our belonging.

WÂWÂŠTESKWAN THE SPIRITS DANCING

Wâciye, hello, my Cree
grandmothers
Tonight in the sky,
I see the wâwâšteskwan,
the aurora,
the spirits dancing,
not normally seen this far south,
welcoming loved ones into the
spirit world.
Mîkwec, thank you, my Cree
grandfathers,
for wâwâšteskwan, the spirits dancing,
of loved ones visiting us on
this side,
spirits trying to reach out to those
they left behind.
I am grateful to
you for wâwâšteskwan,
spirits gone so quickly,
spirits of the dead who remain
in the sky
to communicate with their loved
ones on Earth,
part of the cycle of life.
The stories tell you shouldn't
whistle at them
because they will come take you,
dancing even closer, harder,
brighter.
I will remember to treat them respectfully, manâcihew.
I hope they will not mind though
if I send a little whistle into the
night sky sometimes,
to bid them return south,
so I can feel their presence for a moment.

AUTHOR'S NOTE

Šawelihcikewin (receiving with gratitude and a desire to give back)

Thank you to my grandmothers immemorial, for giving me life, for guiding me before I knew it was you there with me, for giving me the energy to find my way, and for walking with me. You rise in me every time I am drowning. Thank you for everything you kept sacred so it could be carried forward. I walk in your honor. I will keep us proud. hiy hiy

ACKNOWLEDGEMENTS

Grateful thanks to Andrew Mack and Jzurnee Myers for believing in my work, and for their insightful and visionary editing of these poems even as we were all still reeling in the aftermath of Hurricane Helene. I honor also my writing instructor Dana Wildsmith, who taught me that the way to write about the traumatic is to make the language beautiful. Thank you to my husband and my children, born and unborn, who are patient and loving with what I need to say and do in this world.

PLAYLIST FOR THE ROADS AHEAD

Every book carries its own music, and Proud Roads is no exception. Kelly curated this playlist as a companion to the collection. These are artists mostly from the north where climate change is indisputable and is destroying ways of life and taking lives every day.

Howl – Tanya Tagaq, Animism album

The Sea has Spoken – Songs of Water

A Sort of Homecoming – U2

Riot X – D.W. Waterson and Tanya Tagaq

Force – Tanya Tagaq

Wahkohtowin – The Red River Ramblers

Wolf Totem – The Hu

Drops of Melting Ice – Nukariik

Dignity – Bob Dylan

The Family Tree – Songs of Water

Water Prayer Song – Andrea Menard

Keep Us Proud – Northern Cree

Liam Ó Maonlaí – Amhrán na hEascainne | Port Orkney | TG4

Belly of the Whale – Songs of Water

Gula Gula – Mari Boine

Ancestors – Huun-Huur-Tu

Te Awa Tupua (Whanganui River Claims Settlement) – Act2017

Lightning Crashes – Live

Remember Me – Fawn Wood

A NOTE ON THE TYPE

This book is set in **Masinahikan**, an OpenType typeface by Chris Harvey (Languagegeek) designed to support Canadian Aboriginal Syllabics alongside Latin script for languages such as Cree, Inuktitut, and Ojibwe. The name *masinahikan* means "book" in Moose Cree.

The design began as an exploration of calligraphic forms for syllabics and ultimately drew on fifteenth-century serif models to achieve a distinct, highly readable text face.

We chose **Masinahikan** for its clarity at reading sizes and its robust, Unicode-based glyph set that faithfully renders syllabics and extended Latin characters.

We worked closely to ensure that the syllabics and renderings in Moose Cree appear as accurately and respectfully as possible, honoring both linguistic integrity and cultural context.

LOBLOLLY PRESS

Loblolly Press is an independent press based in Asheville, North Carolina, publishing contemporary poetry, short fiction, and novels from emerging and marginalized writers across the American South. We seek out distinctly Southern voices from communities and experiences too often overlooked by traditional publishing, building a community where writers and readers alike can see themselves reflected in the work.

RECENT AND FORTHCOMING FROM LOBLOLLY PRESS

The Surfacing of Joy   Earl J. Wilcox (2023)

If Lost   Clint Bowman (2024)

Distant Relations   Cheryl Whitehead (2025)

Beasts of Chase   Andrew Mack (2025)

The Computer Room   Emma Ensley (2025)

Proud Roads   Kelly Riedesel (2025)

Habitats   Garrett Ashley (2026)

www.ingramcontent.com/pod-product-compliance
Lightning Source LLC
Chambersburg PA
CBHW052131030426
42337CB00028B/5112